The Blessed Path #2

For information address:

J2B Publishing LLC
4251 Columbia Park Road
Pomfret, MD 20675
www.J2BLLC.com

Printed and bound in the United States of America.

This book is set in Lucinda Calligraphy.

ISBN: 978-1-948747-92-9

The Blessed Path #2

Dorothy A. Simms

J2B PUBLISHING

Reflection

To my husband of fifty-four years and my two children who have been such an inspiration in my life. With love and understanding, they have helped me weather the storms in my life. Many of my poems were written as a result of them.

To my family with love and hope, lasting forever.

Table of Contents

Abuse

Endless Fear

There he stood

Surrounded by death

No feelings of guilt one seen

Streets then clean now stained in blood

As though in an ugly dream

As voices fill the air once calm

A mother's scream, with baby in arms

As tears roll down her lovely face

A moment her mind will never erase

She stared at her innocent child

The happiness they knew only memories instead

now she rests in a world without guns

Finding peace and comfort in the Master's Arms

Aging

The Face of Age

When we look at the faces
Of age
We see those
Who possessed wisdom knowledge
Understanding and truth
We peer into the hearts
Of those who lived by faith
And those who refrained from
The many temptations in their midst
They knew
The real meaning of brotherhood
Their examples drew the attention
Of youths of their day
And
The world was better then
the earth gave
The best fruit of its kind

The Looking Glass

Time seems to move so fast
And in my mind a looking glass
Taking me back to youthful times
When life was fun
With love songs sung
At night I'd watch a starry sky
Surrounded by the tallest trees
A soft breeze blowing
A gentle hand to squeeze
Time seems to move so fast
If only it could be
A time of love ,youth and happiness
As in the looking glass I see .

The Works of God

The works of God "s hands
Are engraved
In every living thing
On the ground
And in the skies
In the songs that the red birds sing
The holy works of God
Are on mountain tops
With vines climbing up
From bottom to the top
He has given life to every living thing
and poured out his love
His holy spirit so free
All in remembrance
Of those who are away from thee .

Beauty

Beauty Everywhere

When I was a little girl
I found beauty everywhere
I sat in grandma's old brown chair
so very big and soft,
the happiness I felt when I heard her gentle voice.
I found beauty in an old dark room
with the light from grandma's lantern
there I could pretend
no consequence there after
dressed in an old gray dress
and shoes that stood so high
How great this made me feel
with grandma standing close by

When I was just a little girl
I found beauty everywhere
in grandma's house
an old dark room
and grandma sitting near

Little Red Bird

Little red bird
High up on a limb
What is it that you sing
What joyful sound you bring
Such happiness I feel
Early in the morning

Pretty Brown Skin

A little girl sat so very near
The thoughts she had she wanted to share.
A look into her bright brown eyes
as she gave a big bright smile.
She said she had a little friend
With such pretty brown skin.
different from mine
still I love her so

I will love her wherever we go.
We'll share our ice cream and candy too,
Her shoes fit my feet
and mine fit her too
We must be sisters
I'd sure like to know
I don't ever want her to go
She will always be my very best friend
I only wish I had her very brown skin

Angels Amongst Us

An old man

With worn out clothes

And a sack on his back

No shoes on his feet

As he lived on the streets

With little or nothing did he eat

As he journeyed for miles

Both day and night

He came to a place

Where the wealthy

Laid stake

To welcome him

No one cared to do

But the smile on his face

Was seen every day

For the holy word of God sustained him

Claimed him

To stand for awhile

O that place of rejection

Remembering all that had been told

Wherever you go my angels

Will show the treasures
Deep in your soul
Though riches you do not possess
My blessings more than gold
My promise every lasting
Just listen and know
My love is everlasting

Purple Petals

Looking out my window
drawn to my view
a patch of purple petals
as if they had a clue
Its petals were so small
with stems about to fall
they seemed just to say
I'm glad I came your way.
We rise to the morning sun
and return when noon has come
We live until life is done
we love because your heart we've won

Rise Up

Rise up my love
Don't weep for me
Tears falling down
With your head upon your knee
I'm flying high with the angels in the sky
To the other side
I'll see you by and by.
Rise up oh love
Remember the times we shared
Dancing so hard
Forgetting all our cares
Till the break of day
That old music played
We were so happy
You and I
We lived
And loved
Our way

Rock Of Life

O everlasting rock of life
That's what you are to me
Your loving and caring ways
Touch the very heart

O everlasting rock of life
An example of life at its best
Such strength you have shown
When faced with life's roughest test
You never seem to worry
You said God would make a way
What a blessing
His words are true today

O everlasting rock of life
Mother, that's what you are to me
How wonderful to have
A love that will always be

The Rarest Rose

It comes with the burst of the morning sun
It's petals so beautifully designed
It's fragrance so wonderful
The rarest rose so divine
And as I lifted it from its stem
A vision came to mind
The times you gave words of wisdom
O what a golden time.
Your words meant so very much to me
They helped me along the way
In times of uncertainty
Your words drove fear away
You were there to listen
From a heavy heart I was set free
Like the rose
Such beauty in all I see
Such joy in your presences
O loving
Mother
How special you are to me

Winter

Its days are cold and dreary
So Few flowers bloom
The birds find a hiding place
the trees hang their branches in gloom
The snow comes
What a show, falling all around
as children rush to play
Making angels on the ground
Winter
Blankets gloves and hats
Coats on people, even on dogs and cats
For a season
Then it is through
I see the first sign of spring
A bud peeking through

Morning Sunrise

Before the morning sunrise
I find myself engaged
Listening, waiting with anticipation
Windows open wide
I could hear the singing of birds close by
Their songs filled the air
One far and one near
And I find myself engaged
as the sun fills the room with its warm rays
The softness of the wind
Blowing the curtains in
Drawing them back again
And I find myself engaged
Wanting for just a little bit more
To enjoy

Changing

Flying

Let me soar across the skies
Like an eagle way up high
capturing the view
Of ships at sea
Animals grazing in the fields so free
The warm summer sun against my face
Soaring high
Like the eagle
Way up high

Move on

Move on into the new hour
for that which has passed
can never be
Move on enjoy life anew
and let the morning sun
Set free
A new day
New hope
And a new song to sing

Navigator Of Life

*I'm the navigator of my own life
responsible for my plight
Standing strong in the winds
fearing not the storms of life.*

*I'm the navigator of my own life
for only can I depend
flying with great determination
and believing each flight
I will win*

Childs Play

A Little Boy's Wonder

On a hot summer day
With a clear blue sky
A little boy points
to the birds up high

Their wings stretched out so very wide
clouds that formed mountains with shoes
Flowers wake to the morning sun
Ants whose work is never done

On a hot summer day
with a clear blue sky
A little boy wonders
and seeks reasons why

Castle Of Love

Today they built a castle
with caring, sharing and love
Today they built a castle
where little children hug
where colored blocks are stacked
of red, yellow, and green
in a special way
for this is only child's play
where little ones climb the stairs
inside a castle built so high
where Kings and Queens are born
and little ones sharing happiness
with memories a lifetime long

Memories in the Sand

Today I watched the children play
In sand they built memories to stay
A castle for two
An ocean so blue
How happy they seemed
As their little eyes gleamed
With sand they built a little boat
A pirate in a red and white coat
Who helped them cross the deep blue sea
Where little ones play
On the shore so free

The Making

My little one
I've known you for a short time
Two wonderful years ago
Such a blessing
Sent from God above
As you're watched in your time of play
Your favorite you would choose
The selecting of a special clay
That which God making man used
Though sometimes in your choice of play
I wondered if you knew
That from love
And that special clay
God selected you

Through the Eyes Children

Through the eyes of children
Such wonders do they see
Imaginary friends
with patches on their knees
Shadows on their windows
from branches on tall trees
Thoughts of scary voyages
with blanket covered eyes they squeeze
Then finally sleep comes
and so innocent they become
But for now, their thoughts will rest
until morning
Then with love filled hearts
can little ones express

Discipline

Transformation

As a young child
Mother spoke
And we were transformed
We listened to her knowledge of life
And were captivated by her wisdom
Her rules were stern
With the rising up from her seat
We were transformed
And with time
We learned what it meant
To be young
To be loved
By a mother
Whose rules
Were never meant to be bent

Feelings

Angry Feeling

Anger brings out the worst in us
It drains our strength
It steals happiness
It dims the light in our hearts
It blocks the precious gifts of God

Help

Lord help me
With this strange feeling I feel
Under this weight so heavy for me
Tried so hard, but just can't break free
And all the while
The pain and tears
The screams the shouts
Please stop
Help

Lord, I am just a little boy
Who just wanted a friend
I don't understand what just happened
My thoughts are so mixed up
Help

Lord, I know you see it all
how it damages the minds
Of our children of this day
Help

Madness

Madness does not care
It leaves its traces everywhere
Behind closed doors it silences joy
It changes lives of little girls and boys
It laughs at intolerance
And scrapes at precious thoughts
Leaving behind its traces
Where sanity vanishes
And happiness lives no more

The Choice

With each passing day
Another loved one gone away
Little ones looking on
No respect for mother's arms
Tear filled eyes and painful hearts
To ease their pain where do they start

A young man stood so very bold
no self-respect a stolen soul
in his hands was life and death
Yet only hate could he express
For only in his empty heart
He chose to take
A child of God
A mother weeping
Memories rushing through her mind
Of the love they once shared
gone before its time

Words

Words spoken
Can be a blessing to enjoy
Or a hindrance
Which will surely destroy
The power begins
With the parting of the lips

Which will you choose today

Hope

When I open my eyes each morning
And the sum warms my face
The Robins sing so beautifully
I am reminded
He is in control of everything living thing
It is not I
God is our hope
Our light and salvation
He is our provider
He knows what's best for us
He is faithful
His promises we can trust
When you feel like you are falling apart
Hope
Hope thou in God
His promises are always enough

Hope dies where destruction lives. Let hope live.

Hatred

Prey

It was the dawn of day
I'd worked so hard the day before
This day I longed to enjoy
To the mall I rushed eager to be
Until confronted by an unfriendly three
I walked with elegance proud to be
While being watched like prey from a tree
Swooping down to end my stay
Lord why does this happen so often today
I feel like a bird being chased as prey

Listen

Young man turn around
You're going in the wrong direction
What's that in your hand
You said for your protection
Did you listen to your heart
Why so much resistance
There always is a better way

Young lady turn around
You're going in the wrong direction
Such power in your soul
A shame if it were stolen
Don't listen to the voice
of other's opinions

Just Wait upon the Lord
He is holy and assured
He is the only way
Turn around my friend
Listen to the voice within

Don't just turn away
While hatred steals away
The peace and joy
That's ours to enjoy
If we give our lives to Jesus right away

History

Race

For centuries
We've been colonized, criticized
Hated for our race
Chastised, scrutinized
And told we have no place
Lied about, looked upon
Life seems a sorrowful song
We're bending but not breaking
While history records every wrong

Old Ships

Blood ran thick in those old dark ships
The cry of many
With whips across their hips
Crossing waters
To the land of the free
But instead they felt only misery
Over waters cracking whips
Blood running thick

Blood ran thick in those old dark ships
A certain kind of plan
Sold to the highest bidder
Whips across their hips
Crossing waters
To the land of the free
Not he, she or we, but property

Blood ran thick in those old dark ships
Life knew no certainties
loved ones torn apart
Whips across their hips
Crossing waters
To the land of the free
To the place where freedom was not to be

Blood ran thick in those old dark ships
Over waters
Fearing the sounds
of many whips
Lives that were changed

Seas In Life

Two men sat together
On an old fallen tree
Sharing life's ups and downs
Their struggles in life's roughest seas

From the seas of poverty
Where their feet slipped many times
And with the help of God
even that was left behind

From the seas of racial tension
Which never seemed to cease
They walked with love-filled hearts
Because happiness makes hatred decrease

From the seas where scales are tilted
By man's unjust laws
They learned to be strong
Because weakness causes us to fall

From the seas of being last
When working twice as hard
And facing many mornings
Not knowing where to start

From the seas of family wanting
Where providing was just a dream
The two men had faith in Jesus
Who fulfilled their every need

From the many seas of life
Such men will always stand
Strong with each wave in life
And with faith to call on thee

War

Maybe then we will see
The destruction it has caused

War after war
Fourscore and even more
Men carrying steel
Strapped to their backs
Leading, following
A mission with a cause
Brave, honorable
Some will never see
The sunrise or sunset
For others that died so free

War after war
Fourscore and even more
Men carrying steel
Strapped to their backs
A mission with a cause
Leaving behind a new generation
That will repeat the same

War
Maybe soon we will see
The destruction that it causes

Love

Forever Love

To lose someone you love
Does not bring tears for a moment
or an hour
It is an inward cry indefinitely

To lose someone you love
some may say, "get over it"
or "you must be strong"

But for those who know true love
it is a resting place tucked away
Forever in our hearts

Quotes

Chosen

God knows our destiny
Even before our life begins
How wonderful to have been chosen
By the maker of all mortal men

God

God sustains us
He hears our every cry
He is with us through it all
He will never leave our side .

God's Way

Goodness - in all that we do
Order -   knowing the way
Discipline - being our best regardless of the test

Love

Is not just a word
Or even a thought that comes to mind
It is a place in the heart
It is pure it cannot lie
It knows respect and dignity
Hatred it does not know
It will lead us into unfamiliar places
To save a weary soul

Hopelessness

Hopelessness claims
The dreams of dreamers
Be free to dream

Yesterdays

Your yesterdays are you
Today's distant memories

Life

The bridge of life
Requires daily self -maintenance
In
Love
Respect
Forgiveness
Togetherness
Appreciation, self-control
Respecting each other and preparing
One's self for the coming of our God

Relationships

A Son's Love

Dad you are
A man of essence and equality
The kind of man
You taught me to be
at times when faced with adversities
You showed strength
That encouraged me
You taught me so much in life
Rules to follow
To do what is right
I am so proud to be
A man of equality
Such love will always be
For because of you
Is because of me

A Special Friendship

Though you're gone
Memories live on, memories of you
And the things we used to do
Times when we sat in the summer shade
Grooving to the music
Those from the olden days
Memories of us sharing
The many difficulties in life
You'd say don't worry
Everything will be all right
Tomorrow will be a brighter day
Hang tight and pray .
Though you're gone
Those memories will live on
That friendship we knew
Lived between us two
So when you cross that threshold
Into that brand-new life
Just remember that old saying
Everything will be alright

A Special Grandson

God knew this day would be
and so he blessed the coming of a special grandson
one who would glorify his holy name
one who would do for other's
and expect them to do the same .
one who would speak words of righteousness
one chosen and loved by Thee
A special grandson
whose life I will share
one who warms the heart
and walks the narrow path
Thank you, Lord

Inside Your Heart

If I could see inside your heart
I wonder what I'd see

Would I see loneliness
yet you smile outwardly
Would it be so warm and kind
for this I see in you each day
Or painful memories
that steal your love away
Would it be promises
those never kept
Or would I see darkness
a side that causes doubt
Would I see a light so bright
that fills my heart with joy

I long to know the feeling of your presence
now and a lifetime more

Mother

Full of joy and peace
One whose love is unconditional
With patience
You taught me to be
A mother and friend
How proud to have
The greatest mother of all

Happy mother's Day !

Shared Love

You are the essence
Of the best that life can give
The love we're shared together
Has grown stronger with each passing year
So many times I've wondered
How you knew without a clue
The times I'm feeling lonely
Or when I'm feeling blue
With your warm embrace
You comfort me
You take away my fears
Making me so happy to know
That true love is what we share.

The Question of Heart

As we receive the bountiful

Blessings of God

Do we live with an unforgiving heart

Are we seated next to someone

Who's lonely

And torn apart

Are we confident

That we've done

The holy will of God

As family neighbors and friends

Have we helped

Our fellow man

Words like Water

Words are like water
Spreading miles at a time
Never ending, for they have no conscience or mind
Our words spread, like water
finding the smallest cracks
They can only move forward
There is no turning back

Words once spoken are like water
Some refreshing to hear
So very pure, just the sound of them
feeling its calming flow

Some words that are spoken
destroy the cleanest streams
When in the hearts of those who listened
They cannot be filtered
The stream is never clean

A Lifetime

My life changed
With the echoing of your cry
That special day
As I waited with hours passing by
You came
I knew
I would never be the same
because God gave and we adored you.
A grandson
soon to be a man
Yes, I see
I am proud
Of the person a man to be
And with the happiness that you bring
An echoing cry, long since the day gone by
Blessed by God
Who knows you so well
My grandson now 16
I see the love of God through you

Happy Birthday Alvin

Spiritual Poems

A Broken Vessel

I come to you, O Lord

A broken vessel

Waiting, praying to be made whole again

A wholeness that surpasses all understanding

When your blessings surround me

Your light shines deep within my heart

I thank you Lord

For making whole a broken vessel like me

A Friend Forever

On a warm summer day
not many years ago
a friend came to visit
this friend I did not know
He came and stood beside me
as my eyes filled with tears
He said not to worry
he said not to fear

I wondered how he knew
the sadness I encountered
His presence I felt
Was stronger than a mountain
And though I never saw his face
happiness filled my heart
replacing the sadness
in my soul torn apart

A gift He left to pass along
"I'm with you every day
even until the end of time
my love for you will stay"
Then he turned and walked away
but this friend I never knew
now lives inside my heart
and I see life
with a different view.

A Lovely Time

Such a lovely time, oh Lord
you drew my eyes to see
such beauty on this earth
owned only by thee
peering from my window
as far as I could see
diamonds everywhere
a frosty meadow
a lovely sight
to be seen

Yet I knew such loneliness
a heavy heart filled with pain
until I heard your voice
so very plain
All that you see
is to be enjoyed
on this earth the land
from sea to shore
for every generation

such beauty will always be
to inspire those with lonely hearts
and for those who trust in thee.

A Lost Soul

A lost soul sat at the river's edge

Peering at the beauty it sees

For the first time

It had nowhere to go

It had nowhere to turn

Its true meaning of life

Had been stripped away

And so it sat peering at the beauty seen

It wondered about the many great blessings it had
been given

And the joy that God had spoken to its life

Those that had allowed its seating with dignitaries

Making significant changes in society

It was rich in favor

It had many honorary awards for jobs well done ,

That all changed

With a choice so innocently born

It was calm for a while

Beside the river's edge

It felt safe just being there

And then like a stone being tossed across a mighty
sea

Its ripples carry as far as the eyes could see

And the soul felt its misery

For it came face to face with the life that used to be

And as it sat at the river's edge , it's mind for a
moment was drawn away

It realized that through its own toiling

A stronger force had sat next to it

It spoke newness to the old

Now, becoming Stronger and with favor

he would speak his name to every lost soul

Jesus

Praise , honor, and the victory !

' this rich man had fame , and more than he could
imagine Until he lost it all and discovered what
was missing, Jesus"

Broken Spirit

With a broken spirit
Joy fades away
Loved ones seem distant
Though together yet so far away
At times we feel so weary
And wonder what to do
Just remember that God knows
All that you have been through.
When spirits are broken
And no one seems to care
Just know that you are loved
And broken spirits
Are mended
With our daily prayer

Collective Memories

Oh how I've lived life
Still I haven't lived at all
Only collective memories
When many tears did fall
A heart filled with sorrow
Only came to stay
Never a word of compromise
To start a better day
Oh how I've lived life
When no one seemed to care
Yet I've always thought
That lives were made to share
I only know I tried
To give my heart felt best
Tears keep falling
If only they would rest

Darkness

Oh Lord

Lift me from this darkened place

For light I do not see

This place of pain

And dreadful memories

I tried to find

The slightest ray somewhere deep within

Still darkness stayed seemed endless

My God

For what do I deserve

This place I've known so long

No care or comfort I find

Only hands that push harder

Against the span of time

My God come quickly

For from this place I must be free.

Fallen

When we have fallen
Into the abyss of sin
God protects us
He sends Angels in
They guide us from darkness
Into his perfect light

For All Your Blessings

Dear Lord
Thank you
For Your blessings
Those which you give each day
Thank you for loving parents
Of great morals
With discretion
For little ones to see
Thank you for forgiveness
Where life starts anew
Thanks for my life
For I am because of you
Though at times
I've stumbled
You'd come with opened arms
Knowing all my weakness
You gave me strength to carry on
Thank you for happiness
For peace within my heart
Thank you for correction
and wisdom to guide my way

Thank you for your mercy
And blessings
That never end

Thank you for
Your love
That gives me hope
Along the way .

Glory

To God be the glory
For he has given us this day
To share in all its beauty
Seeing it in our own way
From golden fields to pastel skies
As robins sing their songs
And mothers rock their little ones
Until finally sleep comes.
To God be the glory
For without him no life would be
Sharing in this beauty
And blessed with sights to see
To God be the glory
For he picked someone so true
You are so wonderful
May God's light shine upon you

God Sees

As the night turns to day
And silence slips away
The plight of the sinner's deeds
Are uncovered in everyway
We hear one say
What's wrong with this world today
As innocent lives are torn away
Guns that have no will
Just a man and his plan
Having power in his hand
He chose death over life
How the changes do unfold
For he took the lives of many
Even that of his very own

Going Home

Today two angels came
Their wings open wide
And as they took his hand
They glowed from every side
The clouds of heaven made a path
And light to show the way
To a place of peace for ever
And forever will he stay

Grounded

When I was down
And heavy laden
Only darkness could I see
Grounded by the blows of life
Broken dreams
And misery
Falling lower than the ground
Feeling worthless as I could be
I will never forget
The friend that I met
And for what he said to me
When you are burdened
and others
Seem not to care
Just know that God will comfort you
Just tell it all to him.

Heaven

How much do you want heaven?

Is it enough to change your ways?

Is it more than life's materialistic things?

Or for some who will never have the same

Is it more than those who say?

Separate yourself from that kind

And yet for those who are lost

In other's opinions

God knows their hearts and mind

How much do you want heaven?

For to want is never too late.

Are you willing to help those along the way?

Or do you think that for some

They are just life's mistakes.

Are you willing to walk with

Those who have fallen along the way?

For if just a moment

The very words we share

Could help those who have fallen

On the path to heaven's doorway

How much do you want heaven?

Have you done all that you could do?

How far is heaven?

He left it up to me and you

Homeward Bound

It came without a sound

That calm and beautiful morn

As children started on their way

and mothers kissed them good-by

As Teachers greeted little ones

A lesson they soon would learn

Of hatred at its worst

A new dawn would soon be born.

Yet without a sound it came homeward bound.

Lives lost in a moment

And ashes fall around

As grieving hearts are comforted

And loved ones

Find peace in words shared

As God stood in the midst

Of it all

Lifting his children

To safety

From a deadly evil cause

In Honor of those lives lost in the 9-11 attack

Life's Path

My Lord

As I look at all that thy hands have made

I'm still in awesome wonder

For even the paths that we walk

Back and forth

To and fro, over and over again

Tells a story

A story of life

A story of our own

About our walk

For in sin we walk back and forth

To and fro, over and over, again

My Lord I know a path

One that's straight and narrow

That leads from darkness into the light

A path that narrows as I walk

One with no room to turn around

Thank you for forgiveness

To walk this path with ease

Love to Praise

Up so early in the morning

When I bow my head to pray

O' what a blessing

That God loves me anyway.

He sees through my every fault

His holy spirit is everywhere

On the ground and in the skies

How I love to give him praise

O' so early in the morning

When I bow my head to pray

I thank him for his holy word

Those that help me through each day

He's such a mighty God

His love is everywhere

On the ground and in the skies

How I love to give him praise

Up so early in the morning

When I bow my head to pray

I see the holy works of God

He's so worthy to be praised

Miracles in the Storm

From a distance

I saw the making of a storm

twirling wind and twisted trees

lives changed

broken dreams

Reality moved aside

as disbelief stole its place

eyes looking on

a lifetime of memory

could never be erased

From a distance

I saw the making of a storm

families cling to each other's arms

twirling winds and twisted trees

lives changed

broken dreams

Shelters ripped away while on their knees they
pray

and yet with a new day's dawn

life stood

God's way

For He knew the battles

He calmed the winds

He held your hand

He gave you strength again to stand

But never alone

Mirror Images

Staring in the mirror

Seeing someone I never knew

Looking back at me

Someone without a clue

Someone who needed a friend

a true one so hard to find

One who would speak compassionately

Of the everlasting love of God

Staring in the mirror

Memories of the past rushing back

Those that made me feel worthless

Those that keep me bound

And words of other's opinions

These stole my light away

The image stared back at me .

For a moment

a calmness

filled the atmosphere

I felt peace surrounding me

Pulling away the darkness

A beam of light shone free

Glimpsing in the mirror

I know why

My God rescued me.

Morning Rain

Hope seemed so far from me

As I awoke that day

My mind took me back to happier times

I had what I thought was the best of things

Friends, status

Love, riches

I thought how blessed I must be

Standing tall while others with less

Never measured up to me

I walked past the homeless

And they held out their hands for help

I passed many who just wanted someone

To know the hurt they had endured, from life's
hurtful blows.

I could see it in their eyes

Yet each day I passed them by

Where was the love, so absent from God.

Until that day

From the gutter I lay

Looking out at the morning rain,

that which washed away

Reminding me to mend my ways

From selfishness,

From pride

And the opening of my heart, to the endlessness of God.

No Mistake

Every soul

Was called to be

No mistake of you and me

Oh the glory

I give to thee

On the cross

He died for me

Days have come

And years have passed

Faced with adversities

But carried on

Every soul is called to be

from our sin he made us free

Through God's mercy

His grace he gives

Oh the blood

He shed for me

While I live

I'll worship thee

No mistake of you and me

His holy ways

I strive to be

Oh the glory

I give to thee

No greater love

Could ever be

His life he gave for you and me.

So Many Mountains

Life, what does it mean

For each of us see it

With a different view

Some may feel it to be a true blessing

God wanted it that way

And yet as we awake each day

We have mountains that stand in our way

Those that seem so enormous

Those that cause much struggling

those that are

peaks, and valleys

As we are lifted up one day

And let down the next

During this time

We say when will it end

Only to learn

That on our own we may never win

And when we feel all hope is gone

He lifts us once again

He Watches

As sinners walk on in darkness
Hurtful hearts mourn
God sees the innocent
And those who need reform
He knows those who love him
Their light shines within
God sees the little children
And how their lives are changed
By lustful thoughts and actions
And hearts that know no blame
God watches
He will judge the sinner's plight
Caught in a world of darkness
knowing wrong from right , still God beckons
He calls
He waits
He warns
still the sinner keeps on walking
Caught in a world of darkness
As God waits with open arms

Someone

Someone must have wanted

For he spoke these words to me

Listen closely my child

For my words will set you free

Though you've climbed many mountains

But still have many more

I will be beside you, today and forever more

Someone must have wanted

For he spoke these words to me

Be faithful

Don't give up

I've heard your every plea

Someone must have wanted

For the peace I feel within

O what a Savoir

My Lord my King

My friend

Such Wonders

How blessed

We all must be

Such beauty before us we see

Flowers in bloom

An ever-changing moon

Warmth from the sun

Little ones seeking fun

I wonder how it would be

If Trees were not green

And flowers of one color

Just white and no other

If people of one race

And foods with one taste

With Clothes of one style

And faces without smiles

How blessed we all must be to be loved

To be free

Accepting one another

Regardless of color

It is God's will

As sisters and brothers

The bridge of Life

The bridge of life

Requires daily self-maintenance

In love

Forgiveness

Appreciation

Acceptance

Truth

The Word of God

The Hour

We know not the hour

Or the chosen day

We know not

How many will be called away

We do know

Of God's mercy

How blessed we all must be

Through our darkest hours

His arms comfort thee

We know not the hour

Or his chosen ways

He has given us directions

To help us on our way

Time after time

He has carried us through life's storms

as danger claimed its places

God protected us all

As the storms gave way to a new dawn

We know not the hour

Or the chosen day

We know not why

So many were called today

But God knew

He knows the sorrow

and broken dreams

O children of Haiti

such misery from dust to dawn

Such poverty

To each generation born

We know not the hour or the chosen day

as buildings came tumbling down

And souls called away

O motherless child

Lost amongst the rubble silent forever

Oh Haiti

Lift up your voice in praise

we know not the hour

Or the chosen day

We know

To live is to die

And in times of trouble

Strength will abide

God's promises

Belong to us all

His holy name he hears when it's called

In memory of lives lost in Haiti

But God's joyous welcoming home

The Journey

Before I knew you Lord

You loved me

And I put it on the shelf

You gave me peace

But I looked to someone else

You gave me blessings

those I never knew

You gave me happiness

But from another source I drew

You gave me protection

From danger not seen

You kept me safe

From the world's unfavored scenes

Before I knew you Lord

You knew the person I'd be

And with great distance

I traveled so far from thee

For a while I searched

I found nothing in comparison to thee

For you promised to never leave me

Your truth and love will always be for

Those who thirst for righteousness

For those who call upon thee

The Racer

The racer never looks behind

He is disciplined

He seeks correctness

Assurance is before his every stride

He runs to win

His every step brings him closer to

The yearning that lives within.

And with perseverance

The race he stands to win

Can only be won

Never looking behind

But seeing before him the finish line.

The Trumpet Sound

Oh! what a sound

Just around the bend

A melody so sweet to me

I am in awe

What a sight to see

Angel's wings all around

What a melody

What a sight I see

This must be heaven

For loved one's beckon to me

The Valley

Sometimes in our lives

When we question our existence

We are called to the valley

In faith without resistance

There in the valley

It seems a test of time

Time and time again

In the valley we walk amongst our adversaries

We learn to forgive those who have

Trespassed

Against us

We see destruction at its worst

We know the true feeling of sorrow

And yet as we stay a while

We find the meaning of peace

When we are called to the valley

God knows why we are there

Our eyes are opened

Our souls in full repair

My God, what a valley

Your grace and mercy saved me there

Time

Early In The Morn

What a joy to feel

Early in the morn

To stand

To Walk

To pray

To love

To listen

To speak

To listen to the quietness

To hear the words of God

Ho what a blessing

so early in the morn

when we can share our love for him

and all that he has done

"Hopelessness claims the dreams of dreamers

Be free to dream"

Faded Memories

As I watched the sunset

a rainbow braced by clouds

Such a lovely breeze blowing

across a harvest sky

Leaves of changing colors

a modeled attire each year

An old tree standing tall

with carvings two lovers once shared

A heart with an arrow

A bow forever more

fading just a little each day

like love that lived

but lives no more

Yesterday

I knew you yesterday

I loved you yesterday

You watched me grow

And taught me to know

About life, love, and hope

You knew life and you lived it

You knew love and you gave it

You knew hope

For it helped us through hard times

You knew God

Who said it's time

And he lifted you close to his heart

With him eternal life starts

In heaven is where life will be

Amazed with its wonders

And where life is lived endlessly

Meet the Author

Dorothy A. Simms

Dorothy Simms was born in the month of August 71 years ago in La Plata, Maryland. Her parents, both now deceased, were very stern while raising she and her siblings; with eleven children they had to be. Her home was always filled with laughter and though they may not have been rich Dorothy never felt poor because they made do with what they had. When asked what she wanted to be when she grew up Dorothy remembers only wanting to be a teacher. She remembers lining up the few dolls she had and reading to them.

In August of 1966, Dorothy married and then had two wonderful children. They are now and will always be the joys of her life. In 1967, she was hired as a Teacher's Assistant. It helped tremendously in raising her children to work and have a second income. It also helped her gain the experience needed to become a teacher and then Director. When Dorothy attended college to earn her degree and pursue a career in education, she did not realize she had been blessed with the gift of writing.

In 1989, that changed. That year her writing gift, which had been there all the time, was sparked by a news report that upset her to the depths of her soul. Someone had taken the life of another for a gold neckchain. That gold neckchain sparked her writing journey. Her first poem, *Stolen Hearts and Minds*, has multiplied into over 300, many in this volume.